# Assembly Required

-HOOVES-

A.B.Baird Publishing
66548 Highway 203
La Grande OR, 97850
USA

www.abbairdpublishing.com

This book is dedicated to the ones closest
to me. Your ability to keep me going, on
the tough days, is what made this possible.
So, Thank You.

# Table of Contents

# Love:
-Schematics
-Blueprints
-Technical Details

(Chapter 1)

## 04/03/2019.05:10

To think…

At certain points,
if grasped,
everything could be great:

the creation of a foundation
that wouldn't shiver
when the world creaked.

Things come quick though;
many times a flash in a pan,
definitions in multitudes,
stepping on toes as the setting sits in.

Fear stands with a buffed-out chest
as though time will always last,
whispering, "eventually."

## 03/01/2016,07:38

"Excuse me sir, you've got something on your sleeve. Here, let me. Oh god, why are you bleeding?"

> "It's my heart. It happens when you leave it for everybody to see."

03/27/2019,20:27

I can't take it with me,
so I give pieces of my soul.

Like handing dollars
to the people on the street.

If a piece of me allows you to eat,
I'll give it for free.

Don't ever say thanks.

## 07/12/2018.03:12

I've always wondered
why the best emotions, we declare,
are expected to come from
the bottom of our hearts,

where they are locked away,
buried by everything else
bubbling to the cusp.

Why can't I tell you that I love you
from the very top, the surface,
where it's never been a secret,
easily accessed past, future, and present.

So no, I refuse to love you just from
the bottom of my heart.

It's much too large
just to give you that tiny part.

I'll love you from all the visible edges
that are tangible to thought,
from the corners of the skin
that can be felt with a kiss
to its starving cries when we are apart.

I will love you with the whole,
not a portion of this heart.

### 01/23/2019,07:46

I fashioned her a ring,
one that came from the black mud
that will undoubtedly take us all back,
eventually.

The band was made of chipped and scarred
bone, that once caged my heart
&
will now hope to protect it.

The gems were chiseled from my soul.
The central stone hollowed like my eyes,
smeared a cool blue.

The accents were compliments
to the fear and richness
felt in life.

It was piece by piece
&
now I'm naked,
as you walk around with the
best parts of me.

And you're beautiful.

## 01/31/2019.08:08

Attempts at love have the scent
of a stale cigarette,
lit for the third time in the same day.

You inhale with a racing mind,
imagining all the toxins being drawn
into your life.

Deep into your lungs,
the haze packages your heart
for easy handling.

In your panic,
ideas become decisions
that you can no long snuff out.

You burn.

You burn until scorched fingertips
get their fix,
tossed to the ground,
never allowed to decompose.

### 01/23/2019.19:08

You and I were so young,
popping balloons
&
wishing for another summer sky.

Do you remember how the breeze
cut through the cracked window
as we smoked our cigarettes?

Hand in hand we'd sneak out,
way past curfew,
hoping mischief
held more stories to be told.

We'd dance in unknown driveways
as the moon laughed at us like a drug.

We were the first taste
of the addiction that would come.

## 09/28/2018,21:56

Be good to me and my imperfect heart.
Love me for the beauty beneath this art.

When you find me in pieces,
pick up the sky
before it's completed the fall.
Find me in the darkness
where I crawl, crushed;
show me love, no matter how hard.

If I'm crying out,
give me your shoulder:
it's the doctor's prescription.
Wrap me in your arms
&
keep me from sprinting.
Cherish me
like the masterpiece I want…

…to be

## 11/11/2018.06:34

I am not easy to love,
as though I am the thorns
hidden by the rose.

The idea is delicate;
beautiful as it blossoms to bloom.

I can not be plucked as the others
-the Lilies, the Irises, the Orchids-
when I am riddled with spines.

To hold me,
you must be willing
to search for those few inches
that lay silently for your hands,

the moments of calmness,
in between the defenses I've manned.

## 08/06/2016.07:55

Love is a place we never know
until we create it.

We anticipate its feeling,
its look, and its sound.

But we neglect the weeks, the hours,
and the seconds that are needed
to build it.

We expect it to be sudden,
quick, and intoxicating;
Able to dislocate the heart from the brain,

misconstruing the nature of everyday love.

## 01/28/2019.07:02

I've been staying up
way past an appropriate bedtime,
hoping your shit day
may have become better
&
we could escape.

The silence is a slow asphyxiation,
choking on a tongue heavy with
explanations.

If you only could learn to lean,
to understand others
have trudged through darkness
to better understand how to help you.

I understand it's hard
when the perfume of disaster
still clings to your air.

But there are words that you could hear,
others missed saying out loud
their time around.
Tucked away knowledge
you don't want to neglect.

It's here.

Like changing flowers,
catch them when they are in grasp
or
you'll move on
before the next bloom.

And sometimes these flowers
are only meant for,

You.

## 08/15/2015.Flesh

It's not the Feeling of your touch
      or the Lasing of your tongue
      or the Excitement; the rush.
    It's the Silence that comes
   after two Humans make love.

## 05/28/2017.22:03

Love is not a material emotion
that requires contracts signed in
brick, boards, and stained glass.

Love has no location,
owns no property,
and has no salaries to be paid.

Love is a state of mind.
the heritage of a,
to the death,
partnership.

# Her:
-Missed Steps During Assembly
-Lingering Scents
-Deconstructed Parts

(Chapter 2)

## 01/05/2016.His and Hers

A true love story
that never got to begin.
Each spring they bloom
strictly for them.
The roses were hers.
The violets were his.
They picked a bouquet
for dreams that should have been.

### 06/13/2018.04:36

It's always the sweetest flowers
that get picked clean.

Everyone wants a taste
of just how delicious she can be.

They never stay though,
they get their fill and leave.

There are others drooling
for her generosity.

## 06/14/2018.19:27

She found his heart
pieced together with craft glue.
Chips were missing and white streaks
ran over the parts that took a little extra
work.

It was nothing but a perfect masterpiece
to her.

When their light shown through,
the colors were a vibrant style of true.
The shine didn't leave her blind,
rather it left her sight
with kaleidoscope eyes.

## 05/23/2016,20:04

She was everything right
    but
        nothing he needs.

So on their last day
        his lips dripped with
                bitter dreams:

"I will love you for always,
but happiness will be found
in someone other than me."

## 11/24/2016.21:05

Her tongue tingles
on the sensation
of his claws.

Tracing the gust of air
as he flutters by,

she knows she shouldn't chase
the whisper of his wind,
but her soul's twisted…
Burning again.

She leaps from heights
of which she could never
picture the edge.

Plummeting.

Hoping to fly… being with him.

## 08/07/2015.Hesitation

His past terrified her,
        leaving weak knees and trembling
        hands.

Her future petrified him,
        locking his tongue and creating an
        overwrought regard.

Both hesitating,
        contemplating the odds,
                leaving with imperfect hearts.

## 08/10/2015.Burned Horizon

With a color not many provoke,
she took that plunge,
into a world she knew nothing of.

Emotions over whelmed
by the consciousness of touch,

torched her sky for eternity.

## 01/07/2016.20:29

His lips were always laced
with whiskey and cigarettes.

His hands were sore, callused, and cracked.

His voice was rough and direct.

But she found in him what she always
wanted.

Someone who closed their eyes as they
kissed.

### 12/11/2015.She was...

She was the
perfect illustration
of time.

Toes dipped
in
tangerine sunsets.

Lips always hinting
Of
amber & rose.

A come-on
clear of no.

A gambol
with the genie
in scarlet clothing.

### 03/22/2019.20:36

Every time I see her
it's like the first time.

She draws a hero out of me.

I can feel it
in the wake of her smile.

She makes me want to love her
in new ways,
everyday.

03/20/2019.20:18

There's a magic in her voice,

a certain type of extraordinary
that many don't appreciate in the moment.

They are left to only,
reminisce.

## 01/16/2016,20:44

She is what
you've learned about
in all the stories
&
the reason you can't stop
turning the pages.

## 06/11/2018.08:55

She was the type of girl
our fathers loved
&
our mothers would gossip about.

She had curves you'd never complain
about getting lost in,
with eyes so deep
you knew she held secrets.

You'd bet your soul
she was carved out of ivory,
not fragile porcelain.

It was the subtle things though,
like how she would attack her food
&
snickered when you tried to be sweet,
that were worth mentioning.

Her body wasn't what you needed to know.
It was her soul that never left you bored.

This was not one of those come and goes;
This was what fairy tales hold.

## 01/31/2019.19:36

You puzzled over the consuming scheme
that forced you to play house and had
teachers give you baby dolls.

By 9 you had decided that you figured out
love and it's necrosis.

By the time you reached your 20's
you no longer flinched under the eyes of
old ladies that judged your bare hand,
your empty back seats, or your clean house.

Even when you danced,
you never allowed yourself to remain in
anyone's arms too long. Swirling and
spinning just out of reach of any permanent
creation.

You consider yourself a giant among
tourist. Focused on your business and the
consumption of dwarves. Always pitying
those you were able to step over.

Every time you saw a familiar face
they would seem smaller, more tired, as you
became the maypole they danced around.

### 03/30/2019,16:55

I tried to give you my heart
but you told me no.

You made it clear
you'd rather come
&
get it on your own.

06/24/2018,20:57

I like your anger.
Don't let anyone talk you out of it.

Show passion.
Show you deserve respect.

Show this society
you're more than they expect.

## 02/04/2016,07:16

She whispers in metaphors
because she wants your
conclusions more
than her own.

## 08/02/2016.04:35

She was the
beauty of love
but was afraid
to give it away.

So I traced
the cracks
in her armor
making a wish
every time
she let a star escape.

05/02/2019.18:01

Layers of lavender
roll off of your skin to shimmer
on a sea thick with vagary.

### 12/31/2015.Untitled

She only used her left hand
when she wrote a letter addressed to him.

Because unlike the right,

which had penned
thousands of useless strokes
to expendable suitors,
her left had only wrote for him.

## 11/23/2018,20:59

She was the product
of subtle magic,
the alchemy of starlight,

a supple flower
that bloomed
in the liquid of the moon.

### 01/10/2016.08:26

She longed for the moments
their souls planned for in a whisper.

## 01/28/2019.08:11

Her tears dropped as silent confessions
seeing her death in the depth of your eyes.

Struggling to hide
how she knew this
would be the last time,
she greeted your friends
&
made the most
of the moments at hand.

She knew the morning would rise
bringing a new spot light on y'all's time.

How indiscretions would find another
victim to claim!

### 03/02/2018.22:01

She was one of those women
you don't let slip,

one that smiles next to you,
even in a broke down bed,
sleeping on the floor.

We got a king size today.

She doesn't want me anymore.

## 07/04/2019.10:47

She melts on your lips
like cotton candy sunsets.

Saying nothing
with the execution of her ploy,
she engulfs you.

As the light takes shelter,
she nuzzles closer,
staving off the dark
with her own
obsession of red.

Vibrating a dormant soul,
each tender touch strikes at destiny.

The quivers of the coming thunder,
the foreshadowing of forced pillow talk,
the unspoken promise of an unanswered
question...

"How do you like your eggs?"

# Declarations:
-Fine Print
-Specifications
-Technical Terms Explained

(Chapter 3)

<u>05/01/2016.04:35</u>

Six words to find an end:

I loved you since it began.

## 02/13/2019.20:39

I inhaled you like nicotine,
feeling your grip pervade
&
settle in my lungs.

Becoming my breath,
you infiltrated
&
pillaged my arteries and veins.

The rush was one that came
with no complaints.
The puff, the feeling of each pump,
became the only way I could explain…

How I hadn't escaped.

Oh, did I love you.

I still feel it,
the embers lit and I'm inhaling again.

## 08/17/2019.22:40

I have felt lust,
the quickening of the pulse,
the flush cheeks,
&
the acceptance of indulgence,

the nights of indigo satin lips
shimmering in the saliva of anticipation.

But tonight, odylic, became my taste.
I welcomed the chaotic views,
the random roll of chance,

that tonight was the night I'd find you.

Before my whisper made it through
the clutter in the air, our hands clasped,
iron clad, the perfect settling of
power and exactness.

The vinculum of souls.
The cold moist air on a dry morning.

The disorganized steps of fate.

## 05/30/2018.18:45

I've been sitting outside of your walls
that still stand because of someone else,

wondering how long I'll have to stand
in this cacophony of drenching rain,
until you successfully make
a mosaic of your heart.

I know you're afraid I may find the seams
you believe to be scars,
but I'll let you know
I didn't make it this far
without my own.

If you let me in we can compare
how we repaired each broken part,
finding those places
where they were meant to be
melded together, not kept apart.

## 12/22/2015.But Don't Rescue Me

I've been hypnotized by words before
but I've never been hypnotized
by words never spoken.

But when I peek at your lips
I find myself lost in a sea
where I don't mind sinking.

## 05/26/16.18:36

Please,
show me I'm not wrong for chasing a ghost
of what could be.

Your eyes whisper
what my lips have always
wanted to see.

## 08/30/2017,04:29

If loving you only harbored death…

Well, I've always known I was going to die.

### 07/28/2018.08:47

If I could,
I would pulverize the mountains
to fill with dust the rivers
that keep us apart.

I'd smash the map,
ripping away all the lines
that make the distance clear.

I'd redraw it all
in the image of you
sliding closer on a chilly night.

### 03/08/2019.19:01

She was a whirlwind,
that swept me on a mild night.

Seduced by gentle currents of slowing time,
I found myself captured, deepening,
in her persuasion.

Tossed about in her glowing blues,
the subtle hues, like an exotic perfume,
she filled my lungs with aspirations
I never wanted to lose.

As the night thickened, the moon followed,
as though the spot light was only on her
and I knew it, too.

Unfamiliar faces
became dull and out of focus.
In a way you'd only imagine
happiness could do.

## 01/07/2019.18:21

Do you bring hope or disaster?
Are you survival or destruction?

Darling…

No matter what,
you're a spark for something…
A perfect match…

A means to warmth

or

my own combustion.

I'll either hold the heat melting into you,
engulfed by the scent of a future,
malleable as wax.

Or I could wander the dark,
scorched by the violent abuse,
never able to dodge
the lashings of your fiery tongue.

No matter how the flames taste,
I accept both fates-a paradise or burnt
from the seams.

#### 04/07/2018.12:21

I bloom among the thorns
in order to see how true
your "true love" seems to be.

Are you willing to be poked, pricked,
and bleed for a chance to pluck me?

Are you just another silly boy,
looking to play with something pretty?

**01/19/2016.17:03**

In an orchard of time
where each individual grape
is a memory made,
I want to pick the ones
that will let me get drunk
on ours.

**02/24/2016.19:17**

Oh!
How I would drown in your kiss.

Not
lip to lip
but
lips to every inch we have
missed.

**09/08/2018.20:04**

We stumbled into
our own accidental view
harvesting the moon.

## 05/19/2016.17:02

I'm lost in a world
that's lost in your mind.

I see a future
being lost in our eyes.

Forever lost with you is forever fine.

## 02/22/2016.20:11

As the moon tantalized our room,

I remembered seeing you stretched out
        across the sheets in your
                unspoken beauty.

How delicate I had to be not to tarnish
        your porcelain cheeks.

With each touch, eagerness electrified me.

Tracing the curves of your art,
        I dared not to breathe.

Those moon lit nights were resurrecting.

## 02/13/2019,07:46

We flirted with the sun
but resided in the moon.
engulfed in the effulgence,
it was just you and me.

We tied our tongues into knots;
there was no need to pollute the silence.

As we laid there
roaming through our dreams,
we knew nothing could top our reverie.

When the walls would shake,
we'd hold closer to a requited thought:

"We didn't have everything we wanted but we
had what we needed."

Tears were always brushed away
before they were allowed to fall.

### 01/28/2016.18:32

The night I truly met you,
          you were a wild one.

That wildness only drew me.

It unleashed something that,
even to this day,
I haven't been able to cage.

Some called you crazy,
even too wild to tame.

I just called you mine.

## 10/05/2018,19:57

Through the morning woes,
the sleepy eyes,
and fear of the dawn's cold,
I roll over to find you by my side.

I used to wake up
to catch the luxury of the early sky.
Now, I lay in bed
with you through the sunrise.

Your tender touch, your breath on my neck,
makes me feel foolish thinking
I could ever
find the same thing
in the dancing rain and twirling wind.

Oh, how I ever thought
I could fall in love
without you.

## 02/23/2016.22:35

No kingdom can be complete
without its king and queen.

I need you
like the farmer needs his seed.

Our love will be the rain
that sprouts the greens,
that allows us to breathe
this intoxication of "we."

## 02/12/2016.08:21

Sometimes she's better than sex.
Sometimes we're better mixed,
entangled in something not easy to forget.

I give her a drive,
she blessed me with breath.

## 08/31/2018.02:15

I counted the days
like worn tiles in an empty hall
as I watched the sun dance
with the moon,
the same waltz on repeat.

After each year that passed,
wasting moments
searching for love in strangers,
I would find myself wishing for you.

I had squandered so much steam
dueling with the pressure
of a tick and a tock,
I had forgotten
about the promised workings of due time.

I finally stopped searching,
gave into the weight of waiting,
and now your gentle lips
are my enchantment.

I'm lost in the delivery of your kiss,
with smiles as the lasting remnants.

06/06/2018,18:38

You always worried about how you looked
in your dress or your jeans.

Never realizing…

You looked best when they were crumbled on
the floor sliding in between the sheets
with me.

## 02/24/2016.18:39

I will kiss you from head to toe
just to remind you
why each goose bump has a home.

## 06/10/2018,07:32

Whenever I forget
why I'm always up
with the rising sun.

All I have to do
is look back at that
tangled clutter of sheets
&
your hair in that messy bun.

It's a sweet sacrifice for love.

# Troubleshooting:
-Dimensions and Weights
-Breakdown of Function
-Strange Noises

(Chapter 4)

<u>01/22/2016.03:16</u>

"I leave because I do care about you,
darling. I care about you so much.
I would rather hurt you only once than be
given the chance to do it
over and over again."

## 03/18/2018.23:40

I asked her, "what exactly do you mean?"

She just sat there,
with no rays, with no expression,
just wooden.

She took her fingers,
the ones that always seemed
to be adverse to intertwining with mine,
and ran them down the side
of my pale cheek.

The relationship was no longer new to her.
With each passing day,
as happens with most relationships,
the thrill was replaced
by the chipping of flaws.

Her eyes were finally open
&
they were more beautiful than ever.
I think it's because I could
no longer see myself in them.
The harder I looked,
the easier it became to see
the words to come before she spoke them.

Spilling over her perfectly arched lips,
ones I still vigorously wanted to kiss,
she calmly told me what I expected.
The only surprise
was the amount of time it took to get to
this.

"For no particular reason. I can't explain
it. The feeling that existed. Well, it's
just not the same."

## 01/27/2016.19:59

"Do you remember our first date?
How it ended with thunder and rain?
We should have valued the foreshadowing
that was at play."

## 10/28/2018.16:27

It's a claustrophobic feeling
realizing how things wither away,

how the hours laying awake
talking the sunrise into existence
have now trickled down to a few sentences
you wait on all day.

The sharing of secrets
with the laughter of excitement
seemed like a never-ending novel,
devouring each page faster and faster.

Now those stories sit on a shelf,
collecting dust as neither one of us
can build the want to brush them off.

Even as there are corners of our parchment
that have yet to be touched, we've become
stale to the characters they hold.

We talk about them in passing,
no longer in active.

The flower we opened has wilted.

## 03/27/2019,20:27

At the very beginning
we embraced our bodies as art.

We never found
the correct words that were always aloof
amid the tingle of goose bumps.

We ran fingertips over each other's curves
in a mad rush for love.

But our time was paced too fast
and the days of fleeting seconds
left more questions than to be desired.

Oh darling, what has been done?

Our names in the stories
no longer swing from heartstrings.

There is no more questioning…

We no longer quarrel if the color blue
came from the sky or the ocean.

But we always wonder
what the other could be doing.

We're left with the notion
that our embers could be sparked
once more without spreading.

## 03/12/2019,20:00

I wrote a deft letter
with fragile penmanship
that I tried to mortar
into the fractures
of our home.

I hoped it would explain
why I acted the way I did,
where the failures
in the relationship could be seen,
&
held solutions as possibilities.

But gauging from your posture,
your sunken shoulders with eyes
that refuse to be mine,
you've already packed away your emotions.

Just please, leave the bits of happy.
Don't take those with you.

For the effort it takes to keep love
on the tip of tongues
that are timid in the quakes,

I deserve to live without being

shaken.

## 11/19/2018.11:47

Her laugh,
like confetti,
settled in the nooks and crannies
of my brain.

Brightly colored moments
bled through, stains unfading.

She used to call me babe,
words moist with sweets.

Now she never calls,
her voice, only a memory
for how things could be.

With tissue paper dreams,
I'll never be rid of all the pieces.
They are still scattered in my seams.

## 01/23/2019.06:38

I was like a drunken man
wavering about on weakened legs
reading the dislocated writing
you left on the wall.

You would think I had been blinded
how my fingers traced
the edge of each letter.

Hoping they had more to say,
I was left to hear not just in time,
but in the empty space as well,
the silence had a profound sound.

### 08/04/2016.04:43

Like a fragile sound,
you made a fool of me.

You left me wandering
once I slipped your mind.

I've been sleeping a bit,
restlessly.

With the cold earth
beckoning.

## 03/16/2019,08:48

Nights of hostility
where the truth hangs to the air
with the residue of venom…

Pesky attempts at level ground,
buckled knees
as connections continue firing…

Tortured by the deliberate
attraction of facts to lies…

Do not ask to be pardoned
for the interruption;
there was no similar concession made
when infiltrating peace.

Words are empty enough
to become transparent in the distance
asked of them to travel.

But smile,
drown the questions worth answering.

### 01/21/2019.20:16

You chose not to make me your lover
&
I cannot live as a friend.

So here we are,
spending our seconds foolishly
with nothing left for us to do.

This is the secret of what we are
because of what we could be,

drowning in our attempts
at moving on with our shrinking lungs.

This kiss will never be you.

## 07/02/2019.17:16

Unconsciously,
I continued the compressions
to bring you back;
after the crush of an unexpected wave.

My mind left circling our sunken island,
as though there was still land to "ahoy!"

I can't anchor where we once floated along.

## 02/08/2019.12:45

I was in love
with the ways you'd spread your wings,
how the air would turn sweet
when your lips would make my name.

How brilliant your eyes could be,
generous emeralds that followed me.

You'd hold me closer than most
but only call me friend.

You'd tell me, "maybe in another life."

Sadly, I'm getting tired of dying.

### 01/21/2016,03:01

You've poisoned my heart,
dismantled me far enough.
I never imagined
I'd have to be this tough.

But my blood has become thicker
from absorbing the abuse of your liquor.

I hope you truly love her
because I have never been sicker.

## 12/16/2015.Never I

Always the Charmer.
Never the Prince.

Always the Knight.
Never the Kiss.

Always the Jester.
Never the King.

Always for You.
Never for Me.

### 07/22/2018.19:56

I've left myself laid out
on a platter for you…

Not, once but so many times
that the cool silver became my second home.

Splayed open, my heart exposed
for your fork and knife,
I was never able to fulfill your appetite.

No matter the garnishes of
sweet words I was left in,

There was always a better meal beckoning,
something to leave you licking your lips…

A different dish,
one actually worth remembering.

## 01/24/2019,15:43

We were hopeless romantics
until the bitter end,
worshiping at the altar of today,

toasting our violent incompatibility.

Why didn't you make the bed?
        You were the last one to get up.

The trash is full,
        Don't smash anymore into it.

Didn't you say it was going to rain today?

We never argued about enough though.
We both were entrenched
in the idea of what we had.

Our fights were weekend light shows
where our friends never asked to be
excused.

The passion was enough that they counted
down(if not primed) the fuse.

Our bickering became less playful
&
more of a vulture
darting away only when it felt
a strangers eyes.

We tried to deflect the death
that comes with boredom.

But we were HOPELESS romantics.

### 03/12/2019,19:36

"…and just like that worlds tumble and shake. Towers quake and crumble from mistakes. The best made plans will fall victim to Murphy's idea of the risk it takes."

## 02/03/2019.12:42

The whisper of good luck is muted
with your idea of me being,
"…so fucked in the head."

You always try to shift blame.
your shoulders never strong enough
to hold your own blunders,
as though you were too beautiful
to be burdened with mistakes.

"Remember this is your fault,"
is all you've ever had to say.

It was your last dart to be free,
your last chance to skimp away
without feeling guilty.

I thought we had a chance
but you were too terrified,
pointing out your faults in me.

All I could do was bless your heart
as you argued my love was never more
than a gracious thought.

Manipulation is an explanation for our
love.

## 02/11/2019.19:30

On a twisted axis,
jilted words are spun
into a thread of comfort.

A relief to broken lips,
ideas leaped to heal cracked ribs,
a heart forced to be exposed
has absorbed every thought.

Pointed and punctuated jabs,
finding their mark,
leaving you with familiar questions
that linger through the dark.

### 06/11/2018,06:26

I love hearing that you despise me.
It's my new favorite sound.

It's the only time I've known
you weren't faking,
no matter how loud.

# Scraps:
-Leftover Parts
-Debris
-Maintenance Techniques

(Chapter 5)

## 06/24/2018.21:33

Your impact on someone
does not correlate directly
with the amount of time
you spend with them.

Sometimes the smallest interactions
can have the longest lasting effect,
like throwing a rock into a forgotten lake.

The ripples it creates can reach
from supple shores to rocky banks,
distorting every aspect of what makes
that body a whole
even if that rock was dropped in
at the furthest corner years ago.

When I write about you,
it has been indirect.
It's been in the pieces
&
the fragments of other poems.
I'd use the feelings
&
the thoughts I had
before, during, and after.

I try to remember your swell:
The energy, the speed, the size,
the momentum you created-because
I want to capture that again.

...Even if it's just for a moment.
...Even if it's negative.
...Even if it keeps you with me forever.

## 01/12/2019.17:26

We've always been on opposite sides
in our ideas of eternity.

However,
a connection that has never
needed to be explained
kept us tethered.

With the distance,
I could still feel the heat
from the edge of an embrace.

I still replay the moment I first saw you,
the feeling of my stone heart
chiseled with your name.

As the years have passed,
it should have weathered
but it can never be erased.

A testament to our serendipitous fate.

### 08/15/2011.Who's Dream?

You wanted the college dream.
The drunken nights full of silly things,
flashes pop capturing
every moment hoped for remembering.
You wanted the blackout stories,
walks of shame, tales of drunken glory.
Better catch up and in a hurry,
because the lines in your story
are getting blurry.

01/18/2016,12:02

When you wake,

Please my sweets,
Don't worry about me.

I've been right where
I needed to be,

Loving you,

While finding
Me.

**02/19/2016,12:19**

You were the most vibrant flower
   I had ever found.

I wanted to pick you for my own
   so I could witness your beauty
   all alone.

But love is meant to continually thrive
   and you couldn't do that trapped
   in just my eyes.

So I left you to grow;
   now you're the envy of every rose.

### 08/16/2013.A Simple Search

"I loved her. I loved her with every ounce
of this humbled soul and I think she loved
me too."

"Then why?... Why did you leave?"

"I wish it was that simple. That I just
woke up one day and no longer loved her.
Love's not that simple though. I left
because I had to find out on my own. I had
to decide if the person I was changing into
was who I wanted to be or who I would need
to be to keep a healthy 'Us."

"Well did you find out? Who you were
changing for?"

"Let's just say I found out
it's hard to change regret."

## 06/04/2019,19:41

The bitter taste of sorrow
dwells at the tip of my tongue
as your name stumbles out with farewells.

Drenching an inferno
with the idea of a fools paradise,
an empty room,
left to fill with smoke.

## 01/08/16.17:32

One of my biggest mistakes
is how bad I procrastinate.

It caused me to say "I love you"
after it became too late.

## 02/08/2019.19:54

There's an idea of love that comes
woven in between fingertips
where the grip is often forgotten.

We bank on declarations of forever
when, at its core, has no better chance
than a lasting tide.

Honest mistakes elude the promises that
were made to make them look beautiful.

Now your hollow heart
lets our joyful echo
pass without argument.

When did you fall out of love
with your promise?

Was it when I let you in
instead of running?

### 05/27/2019,20:39

The air was hushed
&
the night was bitter.

Our bed was empty
but
I had to learn to call it home.

The sky could fall
but I would be safe
caught sneaking around in your memories.

### 10/28/2018.18:51

All alone,
I've watched how the world
degrades the idea of "I'll be here."

Oh, how empty words become,
even looking into the mirror,
when the battles have changed.

There's no point to hold back
what you're dying to say;
as the moments slip by,
they care less about what is written.

We've used the idea of what we might say
to destroy us far enough.

…the panic of love.

### 06/11/2018.05:38

I still think about that one time…

How we were right
within our fingertips

we were young
&
didn't understand the stakes.

Now I see you from time to time
&
I have to bury the questions
that flood my mind.

"Have you thought about what if?"
"Am I the only one that still holds that
memory?"
"I wonder if this is that opportunity
destiny gives?"

But you always seem to be doing fine,
that big smile
not hiding behind timid lips.

It's better if I keep this secret.

### 06/04/2019,19:37

The room was cramped with stale smoke and
forgotten advantages.

You walked in on the shadow of memories,
that had burnt to ashes.

No need remembering history.

Your smile sang above the doubt
of a torched out path.

Stay in the Black.

## 01/31/2019,21:17

I'd let her rip out my heart
while it still had a beat,
recognizing the cold of the night air
as she held it in the pit of her palm.

She was the hook I hung from
that I once called pleasure.

Azrael.

## 02/09/2019.20:57

I know you've been drinking.
I remember the taste.
It was a bitter kiss,
laced with recent mistakes.

I know that face,
a smirk forced into a smile,
making excuses for my sake.

All you ever try to do
is sing me love songs,
constantly getting the lyrics wrong.

You rope me in with the promise
of simple talk,
but now you're begging
to stay between my sheets.

Tossing me around with your clumsy breath,
forgetting I am glass.

The moment I shatter, you'll be gone again.

### 03/01/2019.10:22

My fingers betray me.
As I touch another,
I can only feel your body.

My memories aren't a pleasure
but another piece of pain,

a story that tends to be the same.

They are finger prints
on fresh pages
I've already read.

## 02/12/2019,19:07

Waking in cold sweats
from disappointing nightmares,

locked lips repress matters of the mind
with a breathless, "it's alright."

Remember how we could lose ourselves
in each other?

Now the light is shallow, almost darkness.

Straddling the edge,
feeling unimportant,
we knew there wouldn't be a "friends."

We thought at some point
it would come back,
but waiting can be exhausting.

## 04/08/2018,20:27

He has you but he will never have you.

See, there's a difference
between touching a body
&
touching a soul.

He may take you home
but
will he ever understand
the depth of your bones?

He may kiss your lips
but
will you be vacationing
with him in your memories?

I may not have you here
but
I know you'll always have me near.

## 02/09/2019,23:33

I told you I would fight for you
but I'm tired of always picking teeth
out of my knuckles.

You set me up
to be in conflict with my own lips.

You've fallen in love
with the rush of seeing my blood.

Every statement, whisper, kiss,
is another moment you say I missed,
where I'm stuck eating my fist.

Your embrace is demanding of crimson hits

even though,
you'd never allow yourself to be seen
with me as I bleed.

Telling me, you couldn't fall in love
without destroying everything.

### 07/31/2019.17:24

The flashbacks to moments that slipped
carry weighted shoulders and fumbling lips.

The missed kisses, the missed laughs.
The missed tears, the missed spats.
The missed chance.

But I guess this was always the plan.

I was never given the map.

## 04/24/2019,17:47

Not all days are the same;
some come with happiness
but many come with self loathing.

It's a worthless,
misunderstanding of different,
in the same current
but floating along awkwardly,

never in a tangible state to be loved
or express it properly.

Then I have those days of the in between,
where smiles and tears
beg for you to love me.

Why?

Why can't my flaws and quirks be endearing?

Why can't today just be a fact,
that I need you.

YOU...

## 07/19/2016,05:53

I hope you find me
where the heavens blend into the earth,

where gods taste the aroma
of the prairies and the clouds tumble
with the weight of their words.

I will be wading through
the rain and dancing with the firs,

soaked but swinging effortlessly,
spinning and dipping each one
ever so elegantly.

I'll have my eyes closed,
tangled in trusting the wind,

flirting with the horizon
and its growing grin,

all the while tasting the sky
for it hidden recipe.

Licking my lips...
"This is heavenly."

## 03/08/2019,20:32

It's weird…
When you let me down.

I become this other thing.

I become real,
a group of pieces that become whole.

As if I was someone's third wish
that was mumbled through.

A lasting sunset caught in the eyes
that haven't slept.

I become something found in the ashes
of
pleasure and regret.

# Warnings:
-Improper Tool Use
-Chemicals
-Lubricants

(Chapter 6)

## 04/18/2019,21:30

I remember being young,
about 6 or 7,
on hot summer days,
running around the house shirtless
trying to get my parents' attention.

Sometimes I'd catch it for a moment,
a hand or two of old maid,
but mostly they were too busy, "adulting."

They would never say it like that though,
they would phrase it in a cliché
that quieted the questioning.

"You've got to learn how to entertain
yourself, buddy."

I bet if they saw me now,
I'd make them proud.

### 03/13/2019.17:37

There are moments when I wanna get drunk.
  Bring me whiskey and something
  to wash away the remnants.

There are moments I wanna get high.
  Bring me medical so I have an excuse
  for the red in my eyes.

There are moments I wanna fight off
loneliness.
  Bring me delusions of love
  that I won't believe are phony.

## 02/09/2019.23:34

So I keep doing this do-si-do.

I don't know what I want or what to expect.

I've been trying hard, hoping I wouldn't
fall in love with a fling.

I've been trying hard to find nothing.

But I had someone over last night so I
could remember the warmth of a body.

There was no sex. I stole a few kisses but
the intimacy was intimidating.

When I woke up I was plagued with guilt.
I knew her ideas were far from our moment.
It wasn't going to be significant.

I rushed her out quickly.

I've always found my value in being wanted…

I've been trying to avoid it.

## 07/14/2018,12:27

Forgetting beauty can be created
by melting into nothing,
I focus on the chrysalis
painted in over consumption
&
over compensation.

Searching for the joy
some seam out of the
hours, days, and weeks
as they walk around
with their petal to petal smile,
as if their sun is always shining,

finding that silence
is many times the answer
to questions that lack
the courage for asking,
that nightmares are built
from the fragments of broken dreams.

## 01/31/2019,20:48

I tossed my bottle, message in tow,
into the flames dancing gently in the
starless sky,

which casted shadows on woods as my wishes
left them haunted.

With unforgiving secrets,
the heat chases away the cold nights
filled with the cruel idea of how we'd
fight.

As I watch the toxic glass shift
into puddles of light, there is a reshaping
of the idea I've had...

The ideas of...

## 06/04/2019.19:39

Sunny days turn to freight full nights
as the sun sets quickly and the moon jumps
the gun.

Roaring torrents of forgotten behavior
salivate at the processes of your brain.

Whining in the shadows for your two steps
back,

as battles brimmed with belief
shatter on a checkered path.

## Cheap Parchment

I sit at my desk
whiskey in one had
tragedy in the other.
Being careful not to tip my glass again.
I can't afford anymore of this great
parchment.

I sit at my desk
and attempt to write about my truth.
about things I've done,
how a black label has become my closest
confidante.

I sit at my desk,
struggling again.
My hand doesn't move.
the other making quick work
before the ice cubes melt.

I sit at my desk
and drink.

That's what I'll do.

### 04/24/2018.06:57

It's quite deafening, the drip of a leaky
faucet in a house full of empty air.

The only thing you hear (other than the
cockroaches fucking) is your,
hot drunken breath, on the pillow case you
can't remember ever washing.

Laying in those thin sheets
that should be a six foot layer of dirt,
you're stuck in the cycle
of recounting the same sheep,
begging for your mind to quit running and
to just let you be.

These are times I envy the Catholics.
admit, repent, and wait.

They get to sleep.

## 04/24/2019.17:46

Some sit down and pray,

Begging to understand why their kiss
burns through skin.

I don't ask such questions.

The answer doesn't bother me.

As angels fill my bottles with tears,
they have no wings when empty.

## 03/08/2019.19:19

Time,
to my best belief,
was created to be a grave and I demand
to be defiant.

I chase the reaper
in the shadows of pavement,
I refuse to let death do its creeping.

I close my eyes and wander
into the attitude
of self destruction.

The whiskey pours, the air becomes obese
with laughter,
faces blur from the smoke escaping,
the loss of longing.

Dreams were valued and cashed in.

Take me now before I forfeit eternity.

## 04/07/2019.19:35

Left tiptoeing on a rope
bolstered by electrical power...

Tethered between the idea of a near future
and the crackling of a closer past...

Energized by the thought of the dirty come-
down, I fed on the belief that a day could
never die.

Teeth sunken deep in the crescent mood,
I bolted my dreams to an ebony sky.

With bloody gums and a slurring tongue,
I refused to be a casualty of moments gone.

## 03/12/2019.20:36

I've been finding my sanity
in the intoxications of liquid
gratification.

Oh, how simple the world moves
when swallowing the slowing of time.

The whine of the bar musician only entices
the craving of cannibalistic views,

eating myself
from the bottoms of emotions
to the outermost fringes of bone.

Bad decisions,
coupled with nothing I could do,
make the tears feel at home.

## 02/28/2016.02:55

It was 8:18 when my heart skipped its first
beat.

I can never forgive that feeling,
the stench that dripped from the ceiling;
the air reeked of relapse.

My old "once upon a time,"
my old bewitching fix
returned to call on me again.

Like the fine wine she is,
once the bottle was open
there was no mistaking.

My future was forever hers
for the taking.

I made the fatal mistake
to take her as my leap of
faith.

### 02/15/2019.22:25

I began free-falling without sleep,
finding that holding my breath was equal to
how much I wanted to give.

Nobody could guess
I had become a junkie,
that I traded my sanity for your embrace.
I traded my breath to hang on your next
step.

Addicted to your toxicity,
I clambered for the lows since it made the
highs delirious.

I never wanted to know how easy
the taste of you on me could be forgotten.

So I kept buying ever time you would come
around.

## 04/10/2019,21:07

Silver-tongued with devilish intentions,
I lay the road to love
in the mumbling moments
between the silence of the house band.

As the night groans in its old age,
my malignity of nouns
becomes a matador's cape,
for we all want to go home
feeling as gold.

Wrapped in sheets
as both of our lips drip
in the verbal sweets,
falling deeper into a witching escape,

We demanded the sun stay seated;
the light will show the holes in our
conation.

## 06/05/2019.22:59

The constant shadow
of a beast for gluttony
mars the defining edges of footprints
left in strides towards the better.

Salivating at the chance
to devour another smile,
the acidic drips from her
perpetually prevalent tongue
eats through the well-meaning attempts
to mend history.

Karma seasons an appetite
that is never satisfied
&
lingering ideas are served raw
with claws plunged deep
in to the meat of you,

ravaging.

## 01/22/2019.18:36

A lack of despair can be mistaken for hope,
as though true love can be carried
on the crest of unfavorable clouds.

It's a blooming flower
parched for the water;
Beautiful as it wilts.

I do not dread the days that are to come,
but there is no celebration either.

The strings are plucked by others
&
the music will continue to play.

Doleful are the nights.

<u>02/01/2016,06:35</u>

It was pretty quick

how your eyes
&
the passion in your hips

made getting this whiskey
to these starving lips
something I might regret.

But bad mistakes
made with something like this
carries a weight for which
many still wish.

02/28/2016.18:56

I want every ounce of your bad.
I've been dying to take it by the hand.
Show me what living is once again.

## 03/29/2016,18:14

I sit at a table meant
    for me plus you,

staring into a mirror,
    hoping for the reflection
        of our hue.

But the canvas has become too stale.
    I can't find the right colors.

No matter the mix of drugs and
    new types of lovers,
        I can't find that perfect other.

Nothing could bring you back
    to how we began,
        so I slowly kill myself
            with this whiskey in hand.

I can't die to fast
    if I want to understand.

We make mistakes to realize
the lessons we can withstand.

## 05/22/2019,14:35

Its minuet,
as small as the flutter of butterfly wings,
that leaves me breathless as though
under the weight of atlas.

It comes without warning,
a sudden shock to a usually sturdy system.

I feel it crush,
1, 2, 3, then 14, 15, 16,
till all of my ribs collapse.

Wrapping so closely around my heart
it feels as though it's in the grip
of an insatiable skeleton.

The once protective cage,
meant to guard my heart through this world,
shrinks tighter and tighter with each pump.

Each palpitation becomes a gasp,
insuring I'll be damaged by the end.

You can see it in my eyes,
I've grown tired of the repair.

### 03/20/2019,20:18

While chasing ideas that had no business in
my mind, I lost myself for a short period
of time.

I was lead into a falsehood of a familiar
path, blinded by dopamine and its
exhilarating high.

I stopped chasing the sun, listening to the
woods- I traded that all for the hollowness
of eyes.

But before I could be turned back to ore by
her gaze, I ran off the cliff,
back to the sun's embrace.

### 03/25/2016,22:30

I promised my monogamous girls
that I would never roam.

I promised my promiscuous girls,
in my heart, they'd never have a home.

All those promises
&
I still lie alone.

## 05/27/2019,20:16

Accustomed to the taste of flesh.

The addiction of teeth to lip
has made a victim of my instinct.

Greeted by red smiles
and a tongue exhausted
from the strumming of exposed meat.

The layers found a deeper host,
the taste of bones,
the frame of words that were worth
mentioning.

Dust escaping over newly virgin lips.

## 02/11/2019.04:59

I've met lonely,
it's the debilitating weight of so many
dependent on you.

Everyone you meet is a sin, a tremble, a
taste of pain.

They argue that one day everything will
come their way.

Help.

Help me today.

## 02/11/2019,19:29

I've been dining on the idea
vulnerability bringing people
closer to me,
losing myself in the creation
of a house of cards
I've come to call home.

With my dusty slacks and murky soul
left oozing over paper bones,

I'm alone.

They do not come but rather run
from the honesty they demand
as if the truth tastes different
from the luscious lies
they have become accustomed to.

They disappear like the flickering sparks
of dying light.

My tongue has become a handgun,
dealing with the recoil every time.

<u>05/29/2016.19:07</u>

I went shopping for a heart today,

but I could only find them used.

I guess that's all that is left
        in a world full of fools…

I went for one,
        but I'm sure I'll buy two.

## 01/18/2019.20:40

I know all those places you go to hide,
I've been there too.

You can find my bottle caps
&
the names of lovers
that went wrong on the wall.

We defied gravity.

Some called us reckless,
I believe we fell in love with being young.

## 02/12/2016,19:32

I don't black out.
I find peace in a black label.

# Him:
-Lost Tools
-Broken Parts
-Alternate Instructions

(Chapter 7)

## 06/04/2019,19:38

I can feel my life dripping,
little droplets,
down the drain as it streams away from me,

watching the swirl of essence
escape the hold of my body.

Running toward the unknown,
they are misguided,
unsure where to go next,
but certain in their escape.

How do I hold onto a self
that is not just melting
but dissolving in sight?

How do I animate a body
that's soul is constantly
searching for another place to go?

Do I just keep moving,
letting each step fall like precipitation,
or hold my breath,
damming the coming tides.

Worn down by the distillation.

## 11/18/2018.18:47

You can see the fear
bubbling behind his precious eyes,
his delicate blues
that are as abandoned as they are true.

He's constantly living
in an uneasy equilibrium.

He's constantly retracing his steps,
patronizing his past.

He curses the choices that wake him up
randomly throughout the night.
He always tells himself,
"This will be the last sunrise."

He should have known though,

the world only loses those that are wanted.

You can only be taken early when loved.

## 02/22/2019,20:25

Once I was a young boy
with fingers nail-deep in grease,
44 hours of saying,
"Hi, welcome to Micky D's."

Forced to pay rent while using
the Pythagorean theorem for homework.

I sold my soul to chisel out a $50
so we could have a phone-
not for me to be 15,
but to make sure my mother stayed healthy.

I grew up in toxicity,
a story of a rose off-kilter
but
still blooming.

There were so many nights
of school books at dawn,
other nights of not relaxing
till you were in bed.

I still read with my eyes on the room,
I still work like I'm supporting you,
and
my nails are still dirty from loving you.

## 12/01/2017.21:10

What am I suppose to do
with all this love?

I can't bottle it for later use.
I can't give it to someone else,
when it was created for you.

What am I suppose to do
with all this love?

I can't stop it from eating me alive.
I can't stop it from watering my eyes.

What am I suppose to do
with all this love?

I don't want to just survive.
I don't want to just give it time.

So what am I suppose to do
with all this love?

I guess, just hide.
So that maybe next time,
I'll be something love can't find.

## 12/17/2018,19:04

It's crazy how the roaches scatter
when they see light.

Cooking souls with honeyed eyes.

Always sleeping under the love seat,
neglecting the couch.

Choking like the termites,
swallowing the splinters whole.

Chewing a hole through a loser
whose ideas are burned with helium.

Life?

I'm trying for today.

## 01/16/2018.17:24

I walked in to see you draped in ruby red.
Your fiery hair laid across the edge of a
porcelain pillow.

It was quite a view, one I could only
imagine you'd find in war, where water is
no longer clear but thick with the oozing
of vanishing life.

I was too young to notice the signs,
the subtle tendencies that lead to these
debacles.

All I could do was answer when you called,
the cryptic echoes of your voice in the
tub.

I still feel that frigid room,
its attempt to steal the crimson from your
lips.

I witnessed breath leaking, spilling from
your wrist.

Too young to save a life is how I explain
it today…
That I didn't know what I was doing but I
did it anyway.

I bounded your soul to this world
with the vibrant colors you cloaked me in.

I would not let you escape.
You were not going to leave
for the dark or the light,
while I would be left alone at thirteen
It was only the second time of three,
the third I saw coming.

## 02/22/2019.16:16

Nothing stays how it's supposed to be.

Fire turns to ash.
Waves turn to tides.
The wind turns to silence.
Spring turns to the crunch of what we deny.

What you hold on to,
the memories of what you had,
are also what will never be.

History will find a way to repeat itself
but the ingredients will be different,
just like how it will be perceived.

Stoking a fire,
that will have different flames,
and you've already planned to leave.

Deciding not to listen to the pain
-denying that history and future-
are one of the same.

It's what keeps us here,
what makes it worth being
this plain.

## 03/30/2019.04:25

With nails dug down to the bare knuckles,
the grip won't allow an escape.

The only life known
is a circle of friends that can
leave an empty house to shiver at its
bones.

Lip service is delivered in a manner
where any sound can echo throughout
the tone.

Allowed to be devoured by false ideas of
hope,

this is a one-off, this wasn't meant on
purpose, this wasn't what they had in
store.

Thoughts are left with mud in their teeth,
clamoring to let go,
begging to not be the face painted
in dirt.

## 02/03/2016.17:58

At my darkest times,
I take a stroll through the graveyards.

I do it to remind myself to thank
my steps and others' steps before me
for their time well spent.

## 02/22/2019.06:14

I survive on being a light,
a secret sunrise,
for those I keep close
the ones I call friends.

I fight to be
the laughter
&
the spark
that allows them to paint their art
while all they want to do is devour dark.

But they'd never understand
how I feel, a bottle at 3 am, empty.

When I'm alone,
left with no reason to speak,
silence becomes my worst enemy.
I'm left lifting travesties.
A bolder on angles to slippery for my feet.

Making excuses for mistakes,
old thoughts continue their circling.
Swallowed by the grapevine,
I'm writing in shades of easy escapes.

I keep walking,
path lit by the idea that
I'll become better
each day.

## 06/04/2019,19:45

I've wondered at times,
if the palette for Easter
is drenched in pastel colors
because of the morning sun.

Where the resurrection of beauty
is risen from the darkness
that could bury us
in its tomb.

## 02/10/2016.07:08

Nah,
the best revenge
is salivating.

Give me the world
that's gone blind
from an eye for an eye.

That's a world where
the other senses
become truly alive.

So I'll share in their wine
and lick the remnants
each and every time.

## 03/12/2019,19:35

It isn't easy
to find the truth.

Walking a tight rope that many
wouldn't venture to dare.

Distracted by the music left in the air,
never recognizing the laughter
of sinister actions.

It's easier to believe they are still at a
distance.

But it's hidden right out in the open,
if you realize what to look toward.

From their lips,
you'll find shadows
of what they really mean,
like dreams reflected in winter snow
or
the destruction of pristine.

## 04/07/2016,10:21

I may not have an "S" on my chest
   Or
      a suit of shining armor,

But

I know these shoulders have grown
     stout enough to hold

all of this world's horrors.

### 02/22/2019,16:41

I never fear the torture of the next things
to come.

Doesn't it take punishment to become
hardened and worthy to be wield?

Well…

Walking through fire,
cooled by a tongue that spits out mistakes,
only prepares us for the battles of the
day.

I am no master but my edges have become
sharper than his blade.

My choices prepared me for this,
to slice through the roadblocks that would
force me to stay.

The paper-thin excuses
that used to keep me in place
have become the first victim of my escape.

It was hard for me to imagine,
but I'm happier with you as pieces beneath
my feet.

## 02/08/2019,19:56

When I was younger,
I never understood the old man that cried
while looking at photographs.

I couldn't understand that grief is,
essentially, a god itself
always omnipresent.

Its untrimmed nails
rake the grains found in our character.
The past, present, and future are all
victims to its reach.

I could never understand the old man
fumbling over faded photographs
until my own grief found me.

The knock that is now a familiar sound of
death at the door…
A memory of the nights we spent together…

I could have faced towards the world
naked, assured anyone I crossed would have
understood my madness.

How life is both frantic and delicate,
that we are the squirrel that darts in and
out from underneath speeding tires.

We are the neighbor's dog, hoping to be
freed from our chains.

### 03/08/2019.21:24

I'm never left angry
when opportunity might take
another attempt.

Capturing a new moon
in a used trap.

Revisiting footprints,
to make sure we are the only ones
that have moved.

## 01/27/2019.19:49

Life is all about the unpredictable.

Those whose life has gone exactly to plan
will never understand the magic found in
circumstance.

...the discovery of a rainbow that desires
your sunlight.

...a sky painted with the shades of space.

...the dancing of angels that wear mistakes
as a plait of grace.

**01/20/2016,01:05**

"You're sweet."

"I'm just what an average Joe should be."

## 01/28/2019.07:03

I'm sure this is all a bore to you.
The way your life has unfolded.
A greek tragedy in hand.

   "Oh dear, there is no difference
   Between a 10 lb rock thrown at 20
   mph than a 2 lb rock thrown at 200
   mph."

The only part to fear
is the strength of the surface…
And you're strong enough to withstand both.

## 05/27/2016.03:37

I pick at myself,

petal by petal.

I love me; I love me not.

But no matter how I start,
I always end up having
the perfect amount of petals
to know I love me
a lot.

## 04/02/2019,00:44

To be broken is not a curse
or
a reason to believe yourself ugly.

Look at a mosaic.

If we turn our jagged edges,
matching shattered seams,
we are left gazing upon beauty.

# Hooves:
-Maintenance Records
-Manufacturer Notes
-Troubleshooting Equipment

(Chapter 8)

## 01/25/2016,07:46

"I swear you live in your feels Hooves."

    "That's the only place I want to
    live. To be tossed, swallowed, and
    crushed by their waves sounds
    better than to simply be lost
    wandering the desert plains."

### 03/08/2019.20:28

We waited,
held on,
for an idea of what was before,

never asking why we let it go.

When the hurt is over,
we remember how the love flowed.

We forgot how a good love is worth writing
for.

**07/30/2016,02:17**

I'm not afraid of being alone.

I'm afraid of not being missed
once I am.

### 12/17/2015.Hollowed Soul

Oh how life can shuffle the deck
in your hand.
Without a reason
for you to understand.

You blink, your neck deep in sand.

Cracked skin and frail soul.
Melodies of knocking bones.
Remembering the highs of highs.
Living the bottom of lows.

Can you feel the wind
with a hollowed soul?

## 04/22/2016,06:42

His pen split the air and began to peel
away its mask,

like the whiskey from his father's glass,

exposing secrets that could never really
rest.

He has a beautiful soul
but
is a terrible man.

## Bite After Bite

When I grab a pen

it's a dangerous agreement.

There's demons I have to conjure.

That still want to eat me.

### 03/27/2019.20:01

Take my tongue and split it in two.

As one side drips in honey,
the other licks at a vengeful tooth.

Be careful as you tread
for the line is razor-thin.

From smiling to tears,
those rosy cheeks can come
from the same
flittering ends.

## 02/29/2016,02:35

I have a piranha soul.
I'll eat you alive poem by poem.
All I need is one dip of your toe.

Can you risk being gobbled down whole?
This isn't for the faint of heart;
this is a life for the bold.
You can't just write,
you must bleed your soul.

This is a twenty-four hour disaster zone.

## Time Zones

Sometimes darkness
can bring the most joy.

Sometimes light
can bring the most pain.

In a world
where we are meant
to be the same,

how can there be
two different outcomes
to the time of day?

## Crevices of Midnight

From the crevices of the bewitching hour,
comes a tint that covers the eyes.

It shades the heart and darkens the soul.

With municipals brighter than stars,
eyes mended in obscurity.

They can not, have not, and will not
accept the well-wisher's
illuminations.

Lighter the path
the further eyes
ebb.

A path of gold
only terrifies.

It reflects what the eyes do not
want to trouble to see.

The crevices of midnight
they can be comforting.

## Needle and Thread

I reach into the depth,
with a needle and tonic thread.

In hopes to lace together
the pieces of what's left.

The edges are fragile, crumbling,
but they hold secrets
I always wanted to keep.

Magic ink on cheap parchment
has become the most important
disaster.

## 04/11/2019,18:42

If you took all the letters I've ever
wrote,

those once dipped in sentimental feelings
and the elegant expression of emotions,

you would have

a house easily blown over by a wolf
in a sundress.

If you took all the time I've spent
delicately deciding how much weight
to give these feelings,

the structure in which
I conveyed my idea
but
was trying not to drop
an anvil on your toes,

you would have

a warranted phobia of wearing chocos.

And if you took all the moments
I've ever let pass,

the ones that I convinced myself
would happen again,

you would have belief
that there was no such thing as death.

### 09/01/2015.04:55

Letters left laden with saliva so pungent,
they were yellow edged before
time could soften them…

The words I spilled for you
are now faded and grayed,
as the parchment crumbled
beneath their weight.

The travesty, sweetened by mistakes,
of how delicious eating my words
could taste…

## 07/17/2019.23:17

Through these words I shall live forever.

Beyond the time dimmed eyes
&
the hearts promised to parish.

My soul will be thumbed through
well after I've been taken back
by my mother.

So I season my words
with anger and honesty
rather than taking them with me.

I'd much rather leave
a bit of flavor behind
greasing the finger
of a future of lost hearts.

### 10/02/2019,18:59

I don't know why I ever decided to write. I never showed a talent for it, really, all through school.

I always got my lowest marks in English, and I still don't know grammar. But here I am, writing despite that nothing like this was in my original idea for life.

And everyone asks, why?

The simple but cliché answer is, I fall deeply in love.

And I was told once, in a dusty bar by a woman who was way too old for me, "You love so deeply. The way you tell your stories, even I get Goosebumps. And I'm not even drunk or in love with you." Nancy had a dry sense of humor, like we liked our whiskey.

Later, when I told her I was going to make my writing public, after hours of drinking and debating the principles of current southern hospitality, she launched me with,

"You don't have to be polished, talking with round corners, to be a good writer. All you need is the stamina for rejection and the absolute ability to fall in love, whole heartedly, especially with your vices."

Now, I grew to be a terrible writer but I
fulfilled her instructions of falling madly
in love with a reckless abandon...And damn
if I don't dance my best with these vices,
aided by my choice of blends.

So here we are… just you and me… You're
reading while my hand trembles out truths,
as I am about to lay bare my secrets.

I long ago gave up on absolution,
preferring to replace these written letters
for traditional confession.

But these "vices" deserve credit where
credit is due… thus let me give them their
moments and introduce you to them by name.

The first was Michelle, she was sweeter
than a peppermint menthol at 15. She was a
guaranteed sudden head rush, that smooth
drag, standing 5'7" with doe brown eyes,
carrying a confidence that hung on your
clothing long after the smoke had departed.

The boy in me fell deep into this
addiction.

The first time she reached my lips, rushed
and nervous, it was a perfect fit. I became
hooked on her easy escape, the natural
feeling. The slow deep inhale of a new
flame.

It was so potent, begging the boy to become
a man. But something so sweet must be
twisted to make art; with Michelle my words
had found a foundation, but they were still
garbage.

The picture was almost too perfect, the reflection too still. So I broke the mirror to show the cracks I thought I should feel. Besides, if love is this great, why not collect them all?

So I tried again.

Ladies and gentleman, I introduce you to…

Addison…my lover on the rocks.

The first to make my drunken thoughts become sober emotions. She was the spilled drink, the giggles, the thought "someone else will have to deal with it." Wrapped in a black label she became my blue eyed reprieve.

That polished burn you just can't stop sipping, guaranteed to fuck you up. She became my Sunday mimosas and groggy Monday. She was a bubbly intoxicant that made every one of my words worth reading. Because… she drank until I was left empty. With her every day was thirsty Thursday, guaranteeing drunken mornings.

Those mornings with her were always the most difficult, never truly understanding the feeling.

Do I need to throw up or eat something?
Am I dying or just suffering?
Where's the water?
Can I wash away the taste of a repeat mistake without brushing?

But like any terrible, yet dedicated,
writer would do - I kept drinking.

As my lips were laced with whiskey,
finger tips reeking in nicotine,
I thought "you know what? I'll take
another swing."


Welcome, Jaclyn.

Jaclyn was the rush of everything you've
been sold,

"Oh you gotta try it,"
"I'm telling you, one hit and you'll love
it,"
&
"Just wait till you're done coughing."

She left me just not caring. Burning lungs
exchanged for a mellow pace. And I was her
secret stash, reserved for that private
space. As promised, she delivered one hit
after another.

Until I lost my sense of need for an
escape.

But unlike the others, this vice left with
no withdrawals. No twisted stomach, no
nicotine shakes, just a cold empty to
cradle my days.

You would think I would learn, after all of
this time, to etch the beauty of this craft
and master writing. But I am a terrible
writer, and there are more vices to
explore.

Besides, the end comes on the back of 4
horses
&
tonight this bed won't be empty.

## Author Biography Page

I know you were expecting to flip to this page and find another cliché author bio to quickly skim through and learn all the usual stuff: that my name is Joseph Interligi, I'm 28 years old, and live in a modest sized city in Arkansas. However, if you haven't noticed, I don't do many things by-the-book. Instead of burying you in facts, I thought I'd explain: why -Hooves-.

It took root with my discovery of Tom Robbins's book *Jitterbug Perfume*. One of the main characters is a creature comparable to Baphomet: this creature was a half-man, half-goat who was afraid of disappearing due to no one believing in him. And that, my friends, is exactly how I felt in 2015.

I was torn about releasing my work; caught between wanting to be seen and the fear of how it would be received. Was my writing too awkward and clunky for readers to grasp the ideas I was trying to express? I didn't want to sign the poems with my name, in case they sucked. I wanted, instead, a sign-off that would capture my feelings about my writing.

So with *Jitterbug Perfume* still fresh in my mind, I thought about that disappearing goat-man struggling to hold a pen in his hooves as he tries to put down all the thoughts in his head; but because of his hooves, no matter how perfect it was in his head, it would never come out as he hoped. This was precisely my fear. That fear pushed me to cling to anonymity and what better way to stay hidden than within your fear.

On August 4, 2015 I welcomed the birth of -Hooves-: the awkward, clunky poet trying desperately to find someone to believe in his very existence.

-Hooves-

Made in the USA
Lexington, KY
05 December 2019